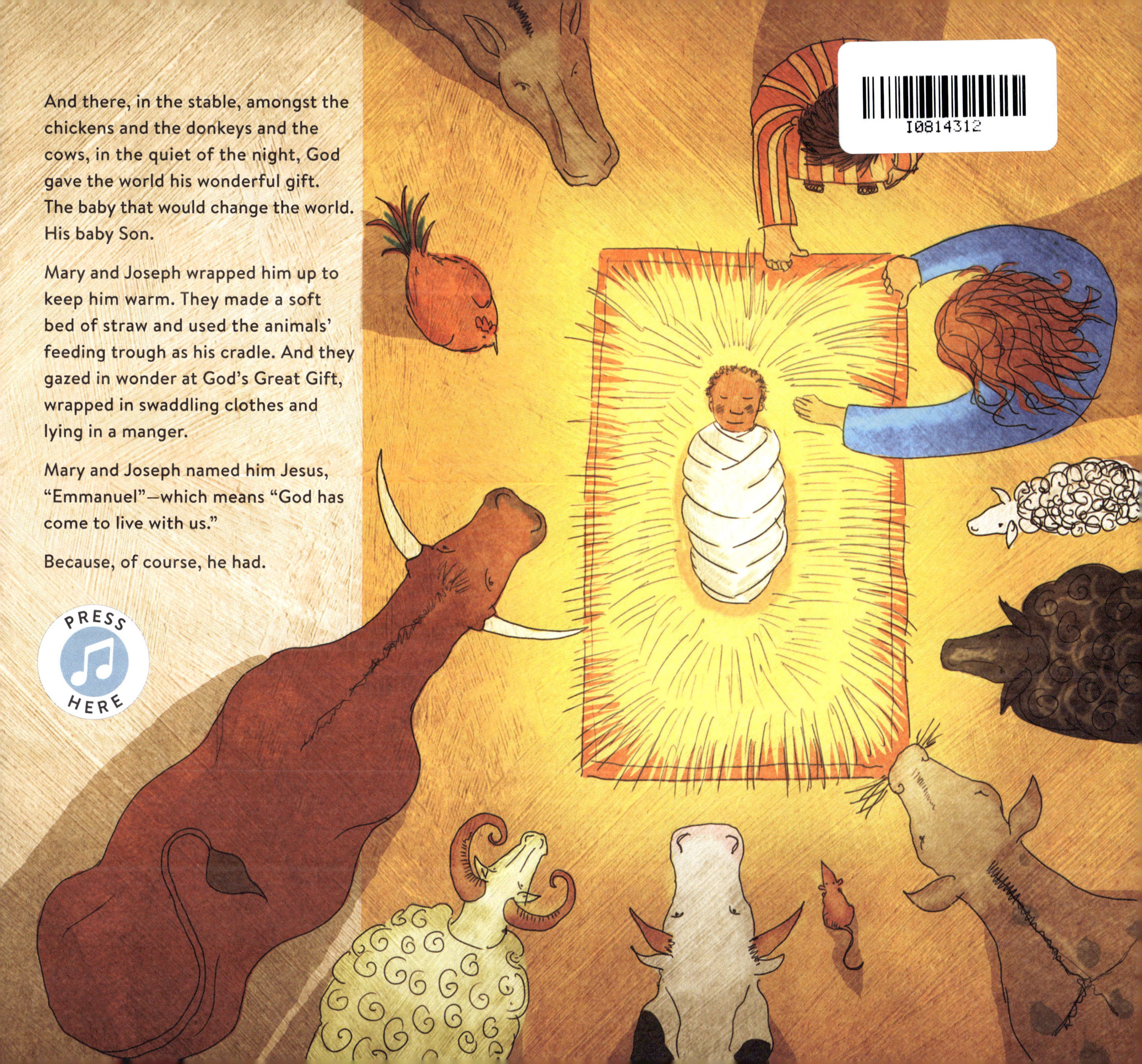

And there, in the stable, amongst the chickens and the donkeys and the cows, in the quiet of the night, God gave the world his wonderful gift. The baby that would change the world. His baby Son.

Mary and Joseph wrapped him up to keep him warm. They made a soft bed of straw and used the animals' feeding trough as his cradle. And they gazed in wonder at God's Great Gift, wrapped in swaddling clothes and lying in a manger.

Mary and Joseph named him Jesus, "Emmanuel"—which means "God has come to live with us."

Because, of course, he had.

THE LIGHT OF THE WHOLE WORLD

The story of the shepherds, from Luke 2

That same night, in amongst the other stars, suddenly a bright new star appeared. Of all the stars in the dark, vaulted heavens, this one shone clearer. It blazed in the night and made the other stars look pale beside it.

God put it there when his baby Son was born—to be like a spotlight. Shining on him. Lighting up the darkness. Showing people the way to him.

You see, God was like a new daddy—he couldn't keep the news to himself. He'd been waiting all these long years for this moment, and now he wanted to tell everyone.

So he pulled out all the stops. He'd sent an angel to tell Mary the good news. He'd put a special star in the sky to show where his boy was. And now he was going to send a big choir of angels to sing his happy song to the world: He's here! He's come! Go and see him.
My little Boy.

Now where would you send your splendid choir? To a big concert hall, maybe? Or a palace, perhaps? God sent his to a little hillside, outside a little town, in the middle of the night. He sent all those angels to sing for a raggedy old bunch of shepherds watching their sheep outside Bethlehem.

In those days, remember, people used to laugh at the shepherds and say they were smelly and call them other rude names (which I can't possibly mention here).
You see, people thought shepherds were nobodies, just scruffy old riff-raff.

But God must have thought shepherds were very important indeed, because they're the ones he chose to tell the good news to first.

That night, some shepherds were out in the open fields, warming themselves by a camp-fire, when suddenly the sheep darted. They were frightened by something. The olive trees rustled. What was that ... a wing beat?

They turned around. Standing in front of them was a huge warrior of light, blazing in the darkness. "Don't be afraid of me!" the bright shining man said. "I haven't come to hurt you. I've come to bring you happy news for everyone everywhere. Today, in David's town, in Bethlehem, God's Son has been born! You can go and see him. He is sleeping in a manger."

Behind the angel they saw a strange glowing cloud—except it wasn't a cloud, it was angels ... troops and troops of angels, armed with light! And they were singing a beautiful song: "Glory to God! To God be Fame and Honor and all our Hoorays!"

Then as quickly as they appeared, the angels left. The shepherds stamped out their fire, left their sheep, raced down the grassy hill, through the gates of Bethlehem, down the narrow, cobbled streets, through a courtyard, down some step, step, steps, past an inn, round a corner, through a hedge, until at last they reached ...

a tumbledown stable.

They caught their breath. Then, quietly, they tiptoed inside. They knelt on the dirt floor. They had heard about this Promised Child and now he was here. Heaven's Son. The Maker of the Stars. A baby sleeping in his mother's arms.

This baby would be like that bright star shining in the sky that night. A Light to light up the whole world. Chasing away darkness. Helping people to see.

And the darker the night got, the brighter the star would shine.

THE KING OF ALL KINGS

The story of the three Wise Men, from Matthew 2

Far away, in the East, three clever men saw the very same star. The star that God had put in the sky when Jesus was born. They knew it was a sign. A baby king had been born.

They had been waiting for this star.

They knew it would come.

"He's here!" they shouted! "He's here!" (And I'm sure if you'd been there, you would have heard them laughing and dancing and singing until the sun came up!)

At dawn, they packed up their camels and wrapped gifts for the baby. They brought their most precious treasures of all: frankincense, gold, and myrrh. Special, sparkly, lovely-smelling, gleaming things—just right for a king.

The three Wise Men (actually, if you'd met them, you'd have thought they were kings because they were so rich and clever and important-looking) set off.

They rode their camels ...

Across endless deserts ...

Up steep, steep mountains ...

Down into deep, deep valleys ...

Through raging rivers ...

Over grassy plains ...

night and day, day and night, for hours that turned into days, that turned into weeks, that turned into months and months, until, at last, they reached ...

Jerusalem.

Jerusalem was by far the most important city for miles around and, as anyone can tell you, that's where a palace would be, and kings are born in palaces. So that's where they went. But they were in for a surprise.

They went to see King Herod. Surely, he'd know where this baby was.

But he didn't. In fact, he didn't like the sound of a new king—it made him cross. He didn't want anyone to be the king except him.

But Herod's advisors told the three Wise Men what was written in their books—what God had said about the baby king: "Go to Bethlehem. That's where you'll find him."

Suddenly, the star they had seen in the East started moving again, showing them the way. So the three Wise Men followed the star out of the big city, along the road, into the little town of Bethlehem.

They followed the star through the streets of Bethlehem, out of the nice part of town, through the not-so-nice part of town, into the really-not-nice-at-all part of town, down a little dirt track, until it stopped right over … a little house.

But wait. It wasn't a palace. And there weren't any guards.
Or servants. Or flags. Or red carpets. Or trumpets. Or anything.
Did they get it wrong?

Or was this what God meant?

Sure enough, in that little house—there, sitting on his mother's knee—they found him. The baby King.

The three men knelt before the little King. They took off their rich, royal turbans and gleaming, golden crowns. They bowed their noble heads to the ground and gave him their sparkling treasures.

The journey that had begun so many centuries before had led three Wise Men here. To a little town. To a little house. To a little child.

To the King God had promised David all those years before.

But this child was a new kind of king. Though he was the Prince of Heaven, he had become poor. Though he was the Mighty God, he had become a helpless baby. This king hadn't come to be the boss. He had come to be a servant.

DECEMBER 1

The Story and The Song

The Heavens tell about the glory of God. The skies show that his hands created them. Day after day they speak about it. Night after night they make it known.

PSALM 19:1–2

God wrote "I love you"—he wrote it in the sky, on the earth, and under the sea ... Because God created everything in his world to reflect him like a mirror ... And God put it into words, too, and wrote it in a book called the Bible. The Bible is not a book of rules. Or a book of heroes. The Bible is most of all a story ... the story of how God loves his children and comes to rescue them. —JSB

When you look at the amazing world around you, remember—someone even more amazing made it. And he loves you.

DECEMBER 2

The Beginning: A Perfect Home

In the beginning, God created the heavens and the earth ... At that time, the Spirit of God was hovering over the waters. God saw everything he had made. And it was very good. There was evening, and there was morning ... So the heavens and the earth and everything in them were completed.

GENESIS 1:1–2, 1:31A–2:1

So God breathed life into Adam and Eve ... and when God saw them, he was like a new dad. "You look like me," he said. "You're the most beautiful thing I have ever made." God loved them with all of his heart. And they were lovely because he loved them. —JSB

When your parents saw you for the very first time, how do you think they felt? Ask them. God loves you so much more than that!

DECEMBER 3

The Terrible Lie

The woman [Eve] said, "God did say, 'You must not eat the fruit from the tree in the middle of the garden ...'" The woman saw the tree's fruit was good to eat and pleasing to look at. ... So she took some of the fruit and ate it. She also gave some to her husband. ... And he ate it.

GENESIS 3:2B, 6

Sin had come into God's perfect world. And it would never leave. God's children would be always running away from him and hiding in the dark. God loved his children too much to let the story end there. Even though he knew he would suffer, God had a plan—a magnificent dream. One day, he would get his children back ... and one day, he would wipe away every tear from their eyes. —JSB

Jesus is the one God sent to comfort you. You can go to him with anything.

DECEMBER 4

A New Beginning

"My covenant is between me and you and every living creature with you ... Here is the sign of the covenant I am making. I have put my rainbow in the clouds."

GENESIS 9:12–16

"Noah," God said. "Things have gone wrong. People have filled my world with hate instead of love. They are destroying themselves ... and each other ... and my world. I must stop them. First, we'll build an ark. A storm is coming ... but I will rescue you." When the ark was ready, God said, "All aboard!" and Noah's family and all the animals climbed inside. And it started raining. Finally, the rain stopped. —JSB

Rainbows can remind you Jesus loves you with his Wonderful, Never-Stopping, Never-Giving-Up, Unbreaking, Always-and-Forever Love.

DECEMBER 5

A Giant Staircase

The whole world had only one language, and everyone spoke it. … Then they said, "Come on! Let's build a city for ourselves. Let's build a tower that reaches to the sky."
GENESIS 11:1, 4A

One day, everyone was talking and came up with an idea: "Let's build ourselves a beautiful city to live in! … And we'll be safe forever and ever." Then they had another idea. "And let's build a really tall tower to reach up to heaven!" God knew, however high they reached, however hard they tried, people could never get back to heaven by themselves. People didn't need a staircase; they needed a Rescuer. Because the way back to heaven wasn't a staircase; it was a Person. —JSB

Jesus is the Rescuer. He is called "The Way" because he is the way God chose to rescue the whole world.

DECEMBER 6

Son of Laughter

But [Abraham] said, "LORD and King … I still don't have any children. … " The LORD took [Abraham] outside and said "Count the stars … " Then he said to him, "That's how many children will be born into your family."
GENESIS 15:2A, 5

Sure enough, nine months later, just as God promised, Sarah (Abraham's wife) gave birth to a baby boy. … They named him Isaac, which means "son of laughter." … God would do as he promised. He would always look after Abraham's family, his special people. And one day, God would send another baby. … This baby would be everyone's dream come true. —JSB

God's promise to Abraham to give him a baby when he was 99 years old seemed impossible. But it came true. God's promises always come true.

DECEMBER 7

The Present

The angel of the LORD called out to Abraham from heaven. … I am giving you my word that I will bless you … announces the LORD. You have not held back your son, your only son, so I certainly will bless you.
GENESIS 22:15–17

God knew that his Secret Rescue Plan could only work if Abraham trusted him completely. … God wanted his people to live, not die. God wanted to rescue his people, not punish them. But they must trust him. "One day Someone will be born into your family," God promised them. "And he will bring happiness to the whole world." —JSB

God gave Abraham a ram so Isaac didn't have to die. Jesus is our lamb who died for us. He is called "The Lamb of God."

DECEMBER 8

The Girl No One Wanted

The LORD saw that Jacob didn't love Leah as much as he loved Rachel. So he let Leah have children. But Rachel wasn't able to have children. GENESIS 29:31

Someone had chosen Leah, someone did love her—with a Never-Stopping, Never-Giving-Up, Unbreaking, Always-and-Forever Love. And you'll never guess what job God gave Leah. You see, when God looked at Leah, he saw a princess. And sure enough, that's exactly what she became. One of Leah's great-great-great-grandchildren would be a prince, the Prince of Heaven, God's Son. —JSB

Jesus is the Prince of Heaven. He is the young prince who left his palace and his throne and came to rescue the one he loves. You.

Press button 8 in back of book.

DECEMBER 9

The Forgiving Prince

Joseph was wearing his beautiful robe. They took it away from him. And they threw him into the well … and sold him to the Ishmaelite traders … then the traders took him to Egypt. The LORD *was with Joseph. He gave him great success. … Joseph's brothers went down to Egypt to buy grain there. … Joseph said to them, "Don't be afraid. … You planned to harm me. But God planned it for good."*

GENESIS 37:23–24, 28; 39:2, 42:3, 50:19–21

Joseph didn't punish [his brothers], he rescued them—One day, God would send another Prince. … God would use everything that happened to this young Prince—even the bad things—to do something good: to forgive the sins of the whole world. —JSB

Even when you mess up, when you tell Jesus you're sorry, he is kind to you. And will forgive you.

DECEMBER 10

God to the Rescue!

Then a new king came to power in Egypt. Joseph didn't mean anything to him. … So the Egyptians put slave drivers over the people of Israel. … The LORD *said [to Moses] … "I have seen how my people are suffering in Egypt. I have heard them cry out because of their slave drivers. I am concerned about their suffering. So I have come down to save them from the Egyptians. I will bring them up out of that land."*

EXODUS 1:8, 11; 3:7–8A

God's people cried out to Moses to rescue them. And God heard them. He remembered his promise to Abraham. He would look after his people. He would find a way to set them free. —JSB

When you cry out to God, he always hears you. And he always answers you.

DECEMBER 11

God Makes a Way

Then the LORD *said to Moses, "Tell the Israelites to encamp near … the sea …" As Pharaoh approached, the Israelites looked up, and there were the Egyptians, marching after them. They were terrified and cried out to the* LORD*. Then Moses reached out his hand over the Red Sea. All that night, the* LORD *pushed the sea back. … The people of Israel went through the sea on dry ground.*

EXODUS 14:1–3, 21–22

And so, that very night, Moses and God's people fled out of Egypt and out of slavery. They were free at last! God's people would always remember this rescue and call it Passover. But an even Greater Rescue was coming. —JSB

Even when we feel stuck, even when there doesn't seem to be a way out, God will always find a way.

DECEMBER 12

Ten Ways to Be Perfect

The LORD *finished speaking to Moses on Mount Sinai. Then he gave him the two tablets of the covenant law. They were made out of stone. The words on them were written by the finger of God.*

EXODUS 31:18

"I want you to love me more than anything else in all the world—and know that I love you too," God told them. "That's the most important thing of all." —JSB

When we love God, we want to do what he says. But Jesus is the only one who could keep all the rules perfectly.

DECEMBER 13

The Warrior Leader

Then the LORD *said to Joshua, "I have handed Jericho over to you. March around the city once … do it for six days. On the seventh day, march around the city seven times. Tell the priests to blow the trumpets as you march … tell the whole army to give a loud shout. The wall of the city will fall down. Then the whole army will march up to the city. Everyone will go straight in.*

JOSHUA 6:2–5

So it was that God's people entered their new home. And they didn't have to fight to get in—they only had to walk. —JSB

In Hebrew, the name "Joshua" is the same name as "Jesus." It means, "You need God to rescue you." Which is why God sent Jesus. Jesus is God come to rescue you.

DECEMBER 14

The Teeny, Weenie … True King

The LORD *said to Samuel, "Do not consider how handsome or tall he is … The* LORD *does not look at the things people look at. People look at the outside of a person. But the* LORD *looks at what is in the heart." So Samuel … anointed David in front of his brothers. From that day on, the Spirit of the* LORD *came powerfully on David.*

1 SAMUEL 16:7, 13A

"He has a heart like mine," God said. "It is full of love. He will help me with my Secret Rescue Plan. And one of his children's children's children will be the King. And that King will rule the world forever." —JSB

The tiny baby in the manger is God's True King that he sent to the world—the King of Heaven!

DECEMBER 15

A Hero and a Giant

Goliath shouted to the soldiers of Israel. He said, … "This day I dare the soldiers of Israel to send a man down to fight against me." Saul and the whole army of Israel were terrified.

1 SAMUEL 17:8A, 10A, 11

With just one swing of his terrible sword, Goliath could finish the boy off. But David kept going. "It isn't how strong you are or how many swords and spears you have that will save you! This is God's battle. And God always wins his battles." God had saved his people. David was a hero! Many years later, God would send his people another young Hero to fight for them. And to save them. But this Hero would fight the greatest battle the world has ever known. —JSB

Jesus is your Hero who fights for you. And he always wins.

DECEMBER 16

The Good Shepherd

The LORD *is my shepherd. He gives me everything I need. He lets me lie down in fields of green grass. He leads me beside quiet waters. He gives me new strength. He guides me in the right paths for the honor of his name. Even though I walk through the darkest valley, I will not be afraid. You are with me. Your shepherd's rod and staff comfort me.* PSALM 23:1–4

David was a shepherd, but when God looked at him, he saw a king. Sure enough, when David grew up, that's just what he became. —JSB

Jesus is your Good Shepherd who has come to take care of you. You can trust him. He knows what you need.

Press button 9 in back of book.

DECEMBER 17

A Little Servant Girl and the Proud General

But he [Naaman] had a skin disease. Groups of soldiers captured a young girl from Israel. She had become a servant of Naaman's wife. She said, "I wish my master would go and see the prophet ... He would heal my master of his skin disease." ... So Naaman went to see Elisha. ... Elisha sent a messenger out to him ... "Go! Wash yourself in the Jordan River seven times. Then your skin will be healed."

2 KINGS 5:1–3, 9A–10

And so it was that a very sick man was healed—all because of a little servant girl who forgave him. God knew sin was like leprosy. It stopped his children's hearts from working properly and in the end, it would kill them. ... Their hearts were broken. But God can mend broken hearts. —JSB

Bring your heart to Jesus. He will mend it.

DECEMBER 18

Operation "No More Tears!"

The people who are now living in darkness will see a great light. They are now living in a very dark land. But a light will shine on them. ... A child will be born to us. A son will be given to us. He will rule over us. And he will be called Wonderful Advisor and Mighty God.

ISAIAH 9:2, 6

Now, God let Isaiah know a secret. God was going to mend his broken world. He showed Isaiah his Secret Rescue Plan: Operation "No More Tears!" —JSB

The baby sleeping in the manger has many titles. He is our Prince of Peace. The Mighty God. Our Wonderful Counselor.

DECEMBER 19

Daniel and the Scary Sleepover

Daniel was ... thrown into the lions' den. ... As soon as the sun began to rise, the king ... hurried to the lions' den ... he called out to Daniel ... "Daniel! You serve the living God. You always serve him faithfully. So has he been able to save you from the lions?" Daniel answered, " ... My God sent his angel, and his angel shut the mouths of the lions."

DANIEL 6:16, 18–22A

"Everyone must pray—only to ME! If you don't, the lions will have you for their dinner!" Daniel heard this. He knew it was wrong to pray to anyone except God. He had to do what God said—whatever it cost him. —JSB

Just think—the little baby in the manger is the Brave Hero God sent to save us. God sent a baby to rescue the world!

DECEMBER 20

God's Messenger

Now the LORD sent a huge fish to swallow Jonah. And Jonah was in the belly of the fish for three days and three nights. From inside the fish, Jonah prayed to the LORD his God. The LORD gave the fish a command. And it spit Jonah up on to dry land.

JONAH 1:10–12, 15–2:1, 2:10

"Go to Nineveh," God said. "And tell your worst enemies that I love them." "NO!" said Jonah. "Those are bad people doing bad things!" "Exactly," said God. "They have run far away from me. But I can't stop loving them. I will give them a new start. I will forgive them." "I'll run away!" Jonah said. —JSB

Through Jesus, God is telling us, "Even though you may run away from me, I can't stop loving you!"

DECEMBER 21

Get Ready!

"Then you will see that I will open the windows of heaven. I will pour out so many blessings that you will not have enough room to store them. The sun that brings life will rise. Its rays will bring healing to my people. You will go out and leap for joy like calves that have just been fed."

MALACHI 3:10; 4:2B

It had taken centuries for God's people to be ready, but now the time had come for the best part of God's plan. God himself was going to come. Not to punish his people—but to rescue them. God was getting ready to wipe away every tear from every eye. And the true party was just about to begin. —JSB

Jesus wants to fill your heart to overflowing with God's Forever Happiness. It's the whole reason he came.

DECEMBER 22

He's Here!

God sent the angel Gabriel to Nazareth, a town in Galilee. … The angel greeted [Mary] and said, "The Lord has blessed you in a special way. He is with you. … Do not be afraid, Mary. God is very pleased with you. You will become pregnant and give birth to a son. You must call him Jesus. He will be great and will be called the Son of the Most High God. The Lord God will make him a king like his father David of long ago. The Son of the Most High God will rule forever over his people. They are from the family line of Jacob. That kingdom will never end."

LUKE 1:26B, 30B

Remember: Jesus is always with you and you don't need to be afraid of anything.

DECEMBER 23

The Light of the Whole World

There were shepherds living out in the fields nearby. It was night, and they were taking care of their sheep. An angel of the Lord appeared to them. And the glory of the Lord shone around them. And they were terrified. But the angel said to them, "Do not be afraid. I bring you good news. It will bring great joy for all the people. Today in the town of David a Savior has been born to you. He is the Messiah, the Lord."

LUKE 2:8–12

God sent a choir of angels to sing to shepherds when Jesus was born. What did your parents do to share the news when you were born or on your "gotcha day?"

DECEMBER 24

The King of All Kings

After the Wise Men had listened to the king, they went on their way. The star they had seen when it rose went ahead of them. It finally stopped over the place where the child was. When they saw the star, they were filled with joy. The Wise Men went to the house. There they saw the child with his mother Mary. They bowed down and worshiped him. Then they opened their treasures. They gave him gold, frankincense, and myrrh. MATTHEW 2:9–11

Jesus was the king the Wise Men had been waiting for all their lives. So they brought the best gifts they could find to Jesus. What is the best gift you can give to Jesus?

Press button 10 in back of book.

CHRISTMAS IS JUST THE BEGINNING…

Christmas Day isn't the end of the celebrations. In some ways, we celebrate Christmas every single day of the year because our Rescuer has come! But in the days after Christmas there are even more celebrations!

Three Kings Day, or Epiphany, is a holiday celebrated 12 days after Christmas. Three Kings Day is the day many people celebrate to remember the arrival of the Wise Men. After travelling in search of the baby, they arrive and present their precious gifts to Jesus. And the word "epiphany" means "revelation." Jesus was revealed as a king to the Wise Men and the whole world.

In different countries around the world, some people make special cakes just for Three Kings Day. Sometimes a small baby Jesus, crowns, dried beans, or other things are hidden in the cake, and the person who finds the treasure receives a prize!

In some places, people don't open presents on Christmas Day. They wait until Three Kings Day! Children leave their shoes out overnight and, in the morning, find notes or presents tucked inside.

The Four Sundays of Advent

In some traditions, each of the four Sundays of Advent stands for something different, and a special candle, usually part of a wreath, is lit each week. For some families, the four candles stand for the Prophet's Candle, the Bethlehem Candle, the Shepherds' Candle, and the Angel's Candle. Other families might light a candle each week to represent hope, peace, joy, and love.

"God Rest Ye Merry, Gentlemen" may sound like a song about jolly men taking a nap, but "God rest ye merry" is an old English saying that means "God will bring you joy." The first lines mean: God will bring you joy! Don't worry: remember that Jesus was born to save you.

Around the time Mary learned that she would give birth to Jesus, Mary's cousin Elizabeth learned that she would give birth to a son who would grow up to be John the Baptist. He would tell everyone that Jesus was the Rescuer.

Being a shepherd was one of the lowest jobs you could have. Important people weren't shepherds. But God calls himself a shepherd. Isaiah said that Jesus would be like a shepherd who gathers lambs in his arms and gently leads his sheep. And Jesus said he was the Good Shepherd.

"Joy to the World" was written by Isaac Watts, one of the most famous hymn writers ever. He wrote more than 750 hymns! The lyrics are based on Psalms 96 and 98 and Genesis 3, and the music comes from a tune created by George Frideric Handel.

God told his people over and over that he was going to send a savior. There are at least 65 predictions of Jesus's coming in the Old Testament, from Genesis to Malachi! In Micah 5:2, God tells the prophet Micah that Jesus would be born in Bethlehem.

5

God promised Simeon that he would see the Rescuer. Simeon had waited a long time and was very old. When he saw the newborn Jesus, Simeon lifted the baby into his arms and his heart filled with such joy that he sang! His song is called the "Nunc Dimittis" or "Song of Simeon."

The Wise Men went to meet Herod at his palace. Herod's palace was built like a fortress on a high hill with 200 steps leading up to it. It had round towers built into the wall around the outside and inside there were fancy royal chambers.

6

The Wise Men's gifts might sound like strange gifts for a baby, but they were gifts that told who this baby was: gold for a king, frankincense for a priest, and myrrh for a sacrifice. Jesus is a King, a High Priest, and the Lamb of God who takes away our sins.

The song "We Three Kings" was written in 1857 for a church Christmas pageant. It was written so that three actors could sing the opening verse together, but they would each have one verse as a solo before they sang the last verse together.

Each verse of "O Come, O Come, Emmanuel" begins with a different name for Jesus: Emmanuel, Rod of Jesse, Dayspring, Key of David, and Adonai. The song has roots going back hundreds of years and was originally in Latin. The English version usually sung today was translated in 1861.